500 more Heartwarming Expressions

For Crafting, Painting, Stitching and Scrapbooking

by Sandy Redburn

Artwork by Suzanne Carillo and Shelly Ehbrecht

Crafty Secrets Publications
15430 78A Ave.
Surrey, B.C. Canada
V3S 8R4

Disclaimer: The information in this book has been brought to you in good faith. We have no control over the physical conditions surrounding the application of the information presented. We disclaim any liability.

ISBN 0-9699410-9-9   Printed in Canada

Table of Contents · Book 2

Themes for Border & Expression Pages

• •

There is a smorgasbord of creative supplies and helpful aids for lettering expressions onto an almost endless array of surfaces. Check with your local retail stores for products from the manufacturers listed below.

Zig Memory Products
EK Success Ltd
PO Box 1141
Clifton, NJ 07014
www.eksuccess.com

Pigma® Ink Products
Sakura of America
30780 San Clemente St.
Hayward, CA 94544-7131
www.gellyroll.com

Needle Craft Alphabet and Design Books
ASN Publishing
1455 Linda Vista Drive
San Marcos, CA 92069
www.asnpub.com

Oil Pencils, Woodburning Tools, Blank Wood Pieces
Walnut Hollow Farm. Inc.
1409 State Road 23
Dodgeville, WI 53533-2112
www.walnut@walnuthollow.com

Introduction

Here we are back with our new revised Book #2, from the Heartwarming Expressions series. Previously titled 425 More Heartwarmin' Expressions, this second of three books now includes over 500 Heartwarming Expressions along with 40 new border pages!

Studies in global interests and trends show many of us are looking for more simple pleasures in our complex, often stressful world. We have become more focused on our families, friendships, spirituality, values, homes and health. Adding some heartwarming and humorous expressions to our gifts,

greeting cards, scrapbooks, wearables, seasonal and home decor craft projects is an easy and fun way to create more warm fuzzies and smiles in our life and the lives of others.

This book is brimming with heartfelt to hilarious expressions to suit almost any occasion. By using pens and markers, a paintbrush, or needle and thread, you can add expressions to all kinds of creative projects. You can also recycle and transform almost any tired old surface into a treasured keepsake or whimsical feel good statement.

Thanks Are Due

There are many people involved in the creation of this book and they deserve a round of applause and a big thank you! To the many creative souls who passed on their favorite expressions, including Raven Regan, Brenda Rintisch and Margo Helliwag.
To Bev Sundeen for her contributions to the artwork. To Diane at Splash Graphics, Claire Patterson at Webcom, Peter Fiddler, and my mom Rachel Van Tassell for their hard work. Thanks to my family for their ongoing

patience and support, while I spent many months in our dining room in an "endless paste-up party", fitting all the expressions and artwork onto each page. I love doing some of the lettering but I saved all the fancy lettering and artwork for Suzanne and Shelly. So, the biggest thank you must go to them, because their talented hard work has added special personality to every page in this book.

Also, a big heartwarming thanks to you for your support and response to these books. Have fun spreading smiles!

Sandy

Sandy Redburn's dedication to inspiring others' creativity includes writing, publishing and teaching seminars since 1993. As the author of the Heartwarming Expressions Books, Sandy admits to being addicted to creating new expressions but promises to stop now at 500 (actually this book has over 500). She owns three rhyming dictionaries and also loves to use great quotes from Miss Piggy to Shakespeare. She runs her successful home-based business with the help of her husband and three daughters.

Shelly Ehbrecht's speciality is in her wonderful lettering and she has contributed greatly to this book from its birth, helping to make it all possible. Shelly has received her CPD, (Certified Professional Demonstrators Diploma) and enjoys teaching folk art painting classes. She is also a full time registered nurse on a maternity ward and lives a happy and busy life with her husband and two daughters.

Suzanne Carillo is a multi-talented artist who was brought on board in 1999 to help with the illustrations and artistic lettering in this book. Now in this revised edition Suzanne's whimsical and humorous artwork and hand lettering grace so many pages, her name has been added to the cover. Suzanne works as a freelance artist.

Easy Lettering Tips & Tricks

Lettering is not as hard as you may think and, as you will see throughout this book, by no means does it have to be perfect or for that matter straight! You can do your lettering by free hand, or you can trace our expressions and designs right onto your project.

If you would like your lettering larger, you can recreate any expression using the enlarged alphabets in the back of this book. You may also photocopy any expressions and have them enlarged or reduced to fit your personal needs.

Trace or pencil on your lettering first, to get your spacing right. A good eraser and see-through plastic ruler are two very helpful tools for lettering.

It's Easy!

1. Use a pencil & ruler. Lettering does not have to be even - just consistent.
2. Hold pens in an upright position.
3. When possible pull your pen rather than push.
4. Add extra embellishments to create different styles.
5. Get bravely creative - but remember practice and patience.

Dot lettering is one of the easiest styles of printing to reproduce. Remember you do not have to embellish your letters with dots. As you will see, you can change your printing style by adding hearts, stars, flowers, snowflakes, holly, stitching lines and more!

There are countless design books available, with wonderful patterns you can incorporate with our expressions. Look around you for inspiration and be sure to read our list of *99 Places To Put An Expression* inside the front cover. Once you start, you will find life offers endless "perfect spots" to add a Heartwarming Expression or tickle some funny bones.

4

Using Pens & Markers

Using Pens and markers is easy and fun because they are now available in a multitude of tip styles, sizes and colors in both water based and permanent inks. Water based pens work well for a variety of paper crafts, but permanent pigma ink markers won't fade and can be used on a large variety of surfaces. The manufacturers of these markers all agree you should hold your pens in an upright position so the tip has full contact with the writing surface. It may feel a bit awkward but will give you the true essence of the pen tip.

You will also find you have better control of your pen when you pull it towards you rather than pushing it away.

Our samples below show how different combinations of pen tips can give your lettering lots of personality and style. They were done with black ink, so imagine adding colour. There are several helpful lettering books available, as well as computer software with fonts that look hand lettered.

Letters - Pigma Graphic 3,
Stich lines- Pigma Micron 01

Letters - Pigma Graphic 3,
Outline - Pigma Micron 03
Stars - Pigma Micron 01

Letters - Pigma Micron 05
Embellishments - Pigma Micron 01

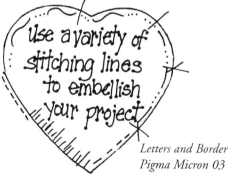

Letters and Border
Pigma Micron 03

Letters - Zig 08 Millennium, Holly & Berries - Pigma Micron 03, Snowflake & Borders - Pigma Micron 01

Creative Possibilities

Photo copying
Our Designs & Border Pages

You can use the expressions and designs in this book as clip art to create album pages, cards, tags, magnets stationary and more. *You don't have to cut the pages of this book.* Please read our copyright restrictions on the first page of this book. For your personal use, have the designs you want to use enlarged or reduced on a good quality photocopier. From your copy, cut out the expression, graphics, border etc. and lay them out on a piece of paper. Attach them with a glue stick, removeable tape or rubber cement. Copy this page onto your final "good" paper or card stock, which you can decorate with colored pens or pencils. You can also have color copies made of your work. Color copies are perfect for scrapbooks, calenders and decoupaging onto projects. Many people prefer to use a light box and simply trace the design they want to use. Anything you want to save for years should be copied or traced onto acid free paper.

Transferring Tips

Depending on your project, you may want to transfer expressions and designs from this book. Once you decide on what you want to use, lay tracing paper over it and draw it out. Lay your traced design on your project surface and slip some transfer paper in between your design and prepared surface. Trace the outline with a stylus or empty pen tip. Saral®

manufactures a wax free transfer paper that works on wood, fabric, metal, glass, tile, ceramic, etc. Wax free paper will not clog the tips of your markers and pens. Heat activated transfer pencils also work well on fabric.

Expressions For Scrap booking & Paper Crafts

You can use our expressions to create your own special occasion and seasonal decorations, birthday cards, scrapbooks, framed calligraphy, greeting cards, gift tags, invitations, stationary and wrapping paper. Jazz up your projects with colored pencils and inks, watercolors, metallic markers, glitter pens, decorative punches and scissors, templates, stencils, stickers, rubber stamps, 3D or traditional decoupage, paper castings, ribbon and more! Again if you are creating anything you wish to preserve for many years use acid free supplies.

Expressions On Wood

If you don't have a steady hand for doing your lettering with a paintbrush, don't worry, you can cheat and use permanent markers. When you apply dots to letters on wood, use paint rather than your pen tip. Not only will you save the life of your pens, you can create dots faster and more consistent in size using paint. Dots can be made using a brush tip, stylus or embossing tool. We use corsage pins and various plastic headed pins for different size dots. Stick the pins into the eraser tip of a pencil and just dip the head into paint. When using permanent markers for lettering, test any varnish first. Krylon manufactures a Clear Matte Spray Finish, which won't make the ink in permanent markers bleed.

Expressions On Fabric

Pre-wash fabric to remove any sizing and don't use fabric softener. You can use a heat activated transfer pencil, or place some fabric transfer paper between your design and fabric (following all manufacturers' directions). Before painting your transferred design, place a piece of cardboard under your fabric surface (a cookie sheet will also work). Use fabric paints or regular acrylics mixed with a textile medium. Look for quality brushes recommended for textile painting, fabric markers, or use the mini tips on paint bottles to do lettering. You can also have a copy centre put your design onto transfer paper, which you can iron onto clothing, quilts, pillows and more. Remember any lettering must be mirrored or it will transfer backwards.

Expressions On Glass & Ceramics

Paint expressions on an assortment of dishware, tiles, glasses, vases and decor. You can use traditional ceramic techniques and glazes, or cheat and use the new glass and ceramic paints. We love the new paint liner pens which are great for lettering. These paints should be baked in an oven for a permanent finish.

Expressions By Needle & Thread

Stitching includes an array of techniques for applying expressions, using fancy threads, floss, yarns, ribbons or beads. Machine or hand embroidery, hand stitching on felt, needlepoint, cross stitch, plastic canvas, quilted appliqués and silk ribbon embroidery are all popular decorative embellishments. You can stitch expressions on everything from baby bibs to bumper pads, decorative pillows, wall samplers, aprons, linens, sweatshirts, vests, jumpers, jean jackets, boxer shorts, ties, bathrobes and more!

The American School of Needlework (ASN Publishing) is a great source for cross stitch design books. They have generously donated the cross stitch alphabets on page 84 in this book. If you don't want to stitch by hand, check out the amazing things you can create with an embroidery machine today!

Embellishing Your Expressions

Depending on the materials and style of your project you can also embellish expressions with raffia, jute, wire, paper twist, ribbons, lace, trims, buttons, charms, shells, fabric motifs, lace appliqués or miniature accessories. To add extra personality to a collection of dolls or stuffed animals, try creating some mini signs to add to the display. You are only limited by your imagination, so go on . . . get creative!

Angels Welcome Here

Angels lend a helping hand.

God Can't be everywhere so He created **ANGELS**

An Angel To Watch Over Me

Do not fear Angels are near

When a child is born an angel sings

Rest Your Wings

There's an angel in each of us.

Grandma's Little Angels Welcome Here.

When in doubt ~Wing it

Angels point the way

Believe in heavenly things

Music is angels talking

Fairy Dust

Fly with the angels Dance with the stars

Nothing can be truer than fairy wisdom

I believe in fairies

Magic happens to those who believe in fairies

9

Our Baby

Worth the Wait

Heaven's Gift

With every little baby's birth
God sends his love and joy to earth.

A bundle of joy...
our little boy

I'm a Dream Come True

Special Things Come In Small Packages

Shhh... Baby's Dreaming

You've Got The Cutest Little ♥ Baby Face ♥

I'm GOO GOO Over You!

Sweet Dreams
Sleep Tight
We Love You
Goodnight

The angels danced the day you were born

Babies Rule!

PARENTHOOD IS A HEIR RAISING EXPERIENCE

Small wonders bring special joys!

Sent From Above (a) our sweet bundle of Love

A baby brings a little bit of heaven down to earth.

The Brightest Love Shines From Up Above

God Rest Your Love Upon This Door
&
Bless This Home Forever More

Blessings

Be a living expression of God's kindness
- Mother Teresa

Whenever I count my blessings you're on my list

Count Your Blessings Instead of Sheep

I love God
and God loves me
God bless my family
and God bless me

Dear God and angels up above
Please bless this home with lots of love.

Bless this Home & all who Enter

Thanksgiving should be Thanksliving

Bless all Creatures Great and Small
Help to Protect Them All   Noah & Co.

Bless this Home with Love and Laughter

Prayers go up
Blessings come down

Bless This Home
Oh Lord We Pray
Keep it safe by Night & Day

Bless Your Little ♡

13

Christmas Glows With Love

We Believe in the Spirit of Christmas

The Spirit of Christmas
Warms Even the
Coldest of Days

Winter is for the birds

There's no business like snow business

Snowmen = water retention

Santa Paws

Santa Claws

Yule is Cool

Save Santa a trip~
be naughty

write in chalk "be GOOD DAys" till CHRistmas

Happy Holly Jolly Days

Christmas comes but once a year
So let us gather and make good cheer

May Your Holidays Be Decorated
With Love and Joy

15

There is no time like snow time

Each snowflake brings to mind
How special you are
You're one of a kind

Snowflakes
are
Angel Kisses

CHRISTMAS.....
A Claus for celebration

The Best Gift
A HUG
cuz every size fits
&
exchanges welcome

We Still Believe

Dear Santa
We've left some cookies
for you to eat
So take a wee break
and rest your feet

Merry
Kissmas

Have a COOL Christmas

LOVE
was born on
Christmas
morning

Christmas ..a very Santa-mental time

Christmas Cheer "Reins" Here

My ♡ Belongs
to Santa

Mittens, mittens everywhere
But never can we find a pair

17

♥ GONE COUNTRY ♥

Good Moos Welcome Here

"Country"

Cow country Watch your step

Keep your sunny side up

Blaze your own trail

Welcome to the Country Club

Hitch your wagon to a Star
-Ralph Waldo Emerson

Never judge a day by the weather

Never squat with yer spurs on

Were you raised in a barn?

My Heart is Udderly Country

Mind your pa and ma

A farmer is a man Outstanding in his field

100% PURE Country

Barnyard Buddies

Ya'll come back now ya hear

19

Ruler of the Roost

This place is for the birds

CRITTERS

Welcome To Our Coop

No Hen-Pecking Allowed!

All birdies welcome to our flock

Friendship is me & ewe!

LOVE builds the warmest nests

Ewe's not fat Ewe's woolly fluffy

EVERYBIRDY NEEDS SOMEBIRDY

The Dog was created specially for children He is the God of frolic.
— Henry Ward Beecher (1813-1887)

Feathered Friends Fly Together Thru "Fowl" Weather

I woolly wuv ewe

#1 Doggie Today

CANINE CONDO

My dog isn't spoiled I'm just well trained

My name is No-No Bad Dog, what's yours?

Forget the Dog — Beware of the Owner

Remember.... "Paws" for thought

21

A cat is just a furry little kid

A Spoiled Rotten Cat Lives Here

CRITTERS

"Meow" spoken here

No home is complete without the pitter patter of kitty's feet

To: Mew From: Meow

Cats leave paw prints on your heart

Feline Groovy

Bird & Breakfast

I'm having a BAD HAIR DAY!

CATS ARE BIRD-BRAINED!

FOWL weather is for the BIRDS!

CAT Crossing

Every birdies WELCOME

A Spring Chicken & Old Crow nest here

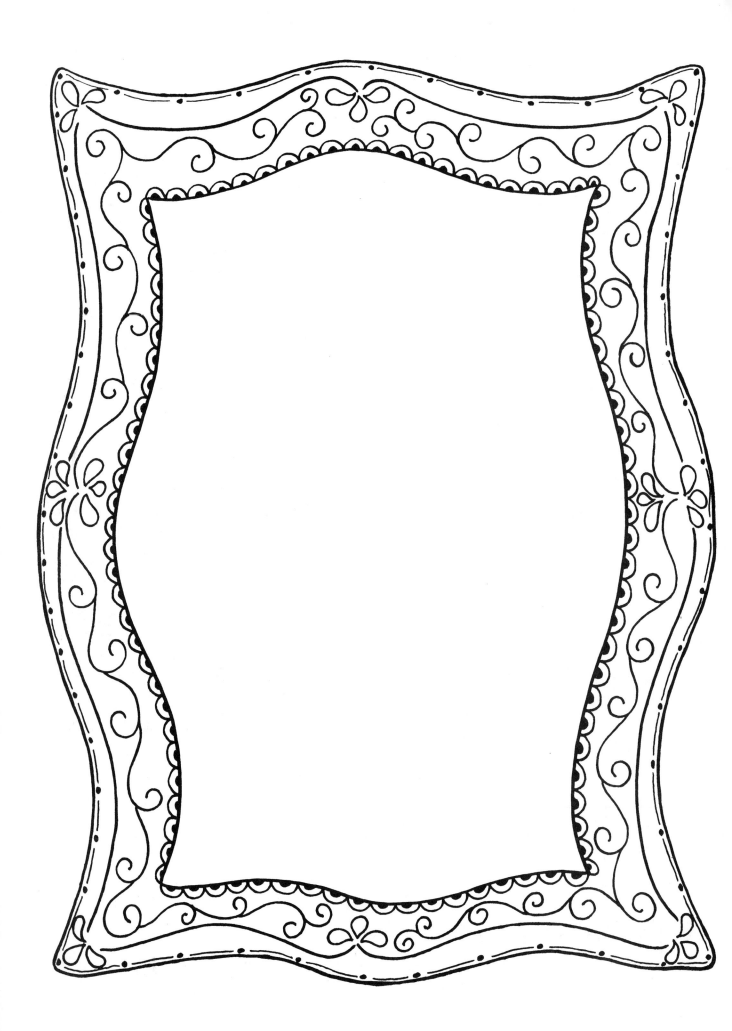

A happy family is but an earlier heaven

- Sir Thomas Brown

Our family is raised on Love

Family

Like the branches on a tree...
a family grows in many different directions

yet will always share the same roots

The greatest gift
I ever recieved
came from God...
my family

Our family tree
is full of nuts

"Our family's Love is tied together with heartstrings"

God couldn't be everywhere so He created mothers

- Jewish Proverb

One thing
so very true
we love being
the parents of you!

ATTENTION ALL TEENAGERS
"NO" is a complete sentence

Insanity is Hereditary....
You get it from your Kids!

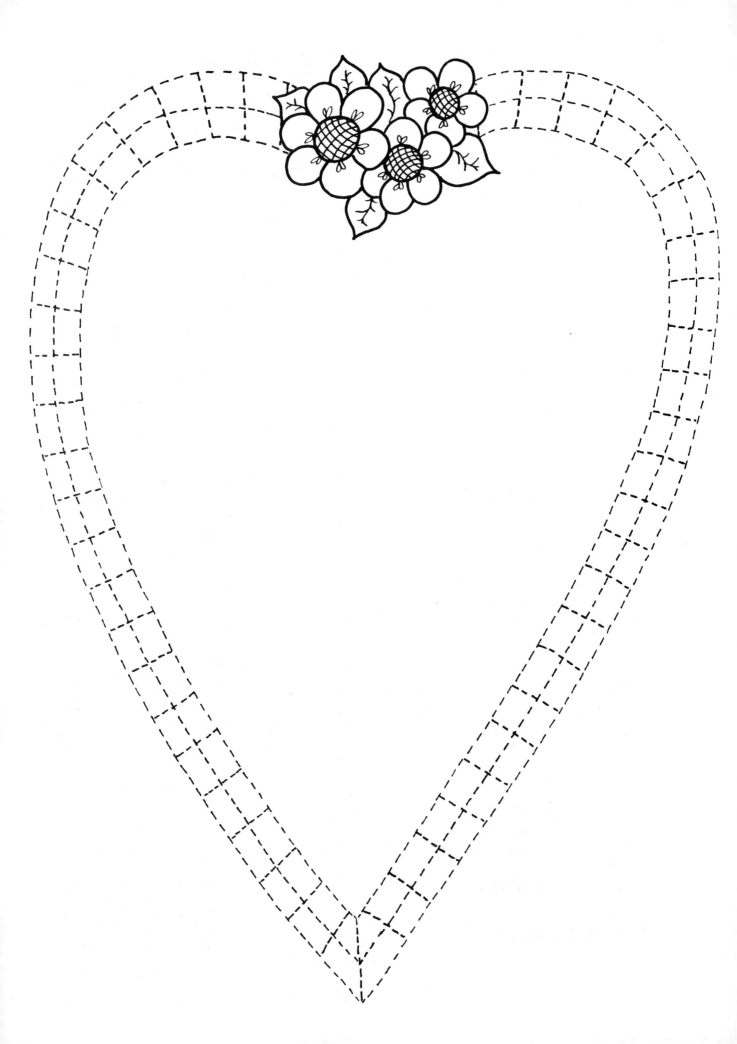

I love to give homade gifts
which one of the children would you like?

Family

SUPER MOM

MOM IS WOW UPSIDE DOWN

We laugh, we cry
We make time fly
Best friends we are
My mom and I !

Mother
Maker of Miracles

All That I Am,
Or Hope To Be
I Owe To My Mother

- Benjamin Franklin

Motherhood : God's highest calling

Mothers do have eyes
in the back of their heads

Motherhood is not for wimps

Mom's
Mood-o-meter
Wonderful
Good
So-So
Ask Dad

FATHERS LIKE YOU
ARE FAR AND FEW...
JUST ONE REASON
WHY WE LOVE YOU!

SUPER DAD

King of the Remote Control

Dad

DADS FIXIN' SHOP
Broken Toys & Feelings
Fixed For Free

My Dad is part
He-man
Superman
Tarzan
and Handyman.
He can even scare away
the Boogeyman!

Someday
I will find
my Prince Charming
but my Daddy
will always be
my King

27

Keeper of Family Folklore & Tales

Family

The best antiques are grandparents.

Grandpa —
the next best thing
to Santa Claus

You put the "Grand" in Grandpa

You can't
Scare Me...
I Have
Grandchildren

Grandmas
are just moms
with a lot of practice

Grandmas are angels in training

For a good time call 1-800 Nana+Papa

Thanx
sista!

Chance made us sisters
But ♥ made us friends.

At first a pesky bother,
now I wouldn't trade for any other
my dear friend ...my brother.

Sisters are joined
♥ Heart to Heart ♥

To A Child, Love Is Spelled T-I-M-E

Wishin' I was fishin'

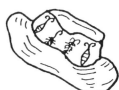

Early to bed,
Early to rise,
Fish all day
Tell BIG lies.

Fish sure grow....
between the nibble
and the time they get away

If this hat's missin' I've gone fishin'

Fishing.....
a reel sport

Fishin' Buds

Fish don't brag
about the size
of fishermen
they get away from

A fisherman
often comes home
with no fish
and a pack of flies

GRANDPA'S SIDEKICK

Born to Fish
Forced to Work

A reel expert
can tackle anything

GRAndPa SAYS i'M A KEEPER

Fishing isn't a matter
of life & death.....
It's much more important.

Fishing Permit Required
But a worm works better

31

People like you are truly rare, because you always listen and care

You are the BEST FRIEND any friend could be, We've shared so many ups & downs You feel like family

One of the blessings of old friends is .... you can afford to be stupid with them.

A Friend Loves At All Times
- Prov. 17:17

"We have been friends together in sunshine and shade
- Caroline Norton

I love all the fun things we do My world is so much brighter Because I'm friends with You

Together or Apart The Spirit of our Friendship Is Always in My Heart

While the Pot Boils Friendship Blooms
- A B Cheales

There is no better looking glass than an old friend
- Thomas Fuller

Only your real friends will tell you when your face is dirty
- Sicilian Proverb

Great Girlfriends Gorgeous, Giggling

When I remember times gone by there's been no friends like You and I

Some things last and some things end but I want you forever to be my friend

33

I Love Friends, Fun & Flowers

A Friend Listens With Heart

Chance made us neighbours but ♥'s made us friends

Friends like heirlooms are special treasures

Like a cup of tea, friends make you feel all warm inside

If friends were roses I'd pick YOU!

Friends make the best collectibles

Friends are stitched Together by patches of Memories

Friendship warms the ♥ and heals the soul

♪ Friendship & Laughter are Music for the soul ♪

Friends like you are precious few

Making a friend takes a moment Being a friend takes a lifetime

Friendship buttons us together.

35

Hand over the chocolate and Nobody will get hurt

Eat, drink and be merry....
For tomorrow we diet!

Broken Cookies
Don't Have Calories

Weight has a way of snacking up on you

Lord help me.......
The devil wants me fat!

DEAR LORD:
IF YOU CAN'T MAKE ME SKINNY,
CAN YOU MAKE MY FRIENDS FAT?

I don't repeat gossip.....so listen closely

I just ate
my willpower

I'd Rather Be 50 Than Pregnant

Star light star bright
Where the heck is Mr. Right?

If they can send one man to the moon,
why can't they send them all?

Sometimes I wake up GROUCHY
Sometimes I let him sleep.

Husband and dog missing,
Reward for dog.

Sometimes the best man
for the job...
is a woman.

SOME DAYS YOU'RE THE DOG...
SOME DAYS THE HYDRANT 37

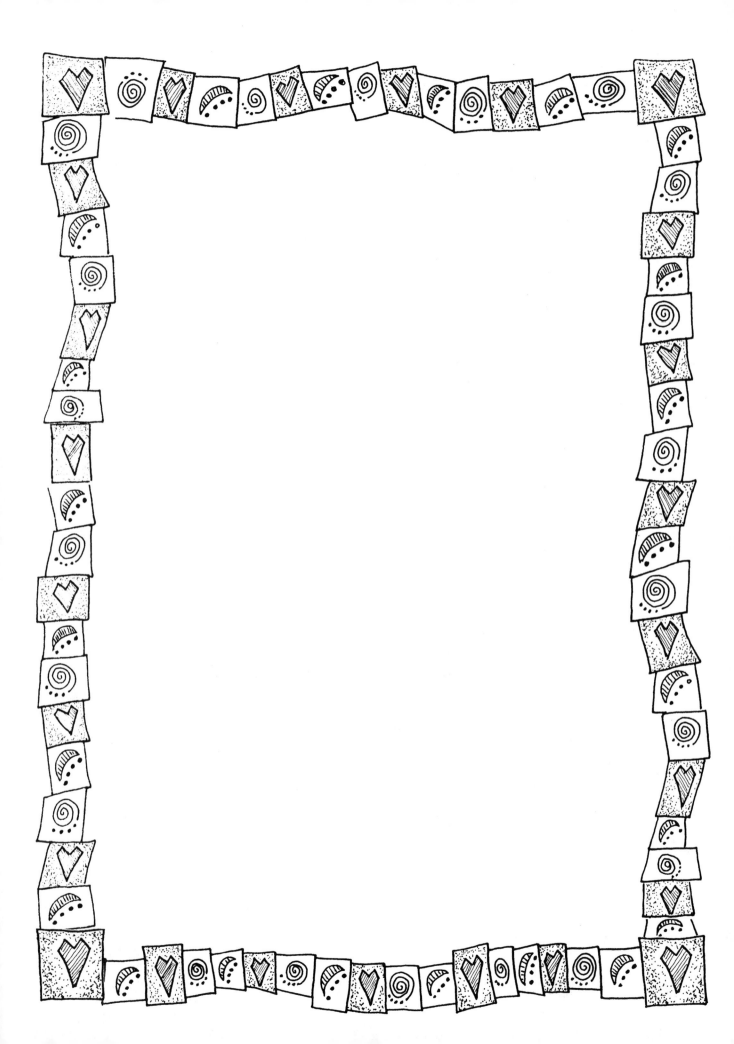

Everyone's entitled to my opinion

"If You Don't Chew Your Food" — Who Will?

Ever stop to think and forget to start again?

I'm in transcendental vegetation

With my luck I'll be at the airport when my ship comes in

I'm not lazy, I'm motivationally impaired

MENTAL Floss PrEVENTs MORAL DECAY

It takes a lot of talent to get a month behind in just one day

Behind every good man ..... is a surprised mother-in-law.

In God We trust all others must pay cash

Madness takes its toll Please have exact change.

God put me on this earth to accomplish a number of tasks.....
I'm so far behind I'll never die.

I can see clearly now... my brain is gone

I'm an Atheist - Thank God

39

Take Thyme To Smell The Flowers

Gardening

Two-lips just for you.

Bless these Blooms

Thyme began in a Garden

What you sow is what you grow

Boss of the Moss

Somebunny's been eating the vegtables

Every bunny Loves a Garden

SEEDS of LOVE

Old gardeners never die They just spade away.

Sow Kindness Gather Love

The only thing I grow in my garden is tired

Sunshine & seeds – scatter every where

Gardening Angels From Up Above

Please Watch Over This Garden With Love

Meet me at the Garden Gate

41

Keeper of the Garden

Gardening

ONE WHO PLANTS A GARDEN PLANTS SOME HAPPINESS

Friends are the Flowers that Bloom in Life's Garden

you make my heart BLOOM

No rain No rainbows

Flowers & Children BLOOM when showered with LOVE

Flowers for Thee With·Love·From Me

I'm in therapy and gardening is cheaper than a psychiatrist

↓ May all your weeds be wild flowers ↓

The Stepping Stones in the Garden of Life
Love Faith Wisdom Joy

MOM'S GARDEN Weed it & Reap

Raised On Home Grown Love

Golf is Tee-rrific

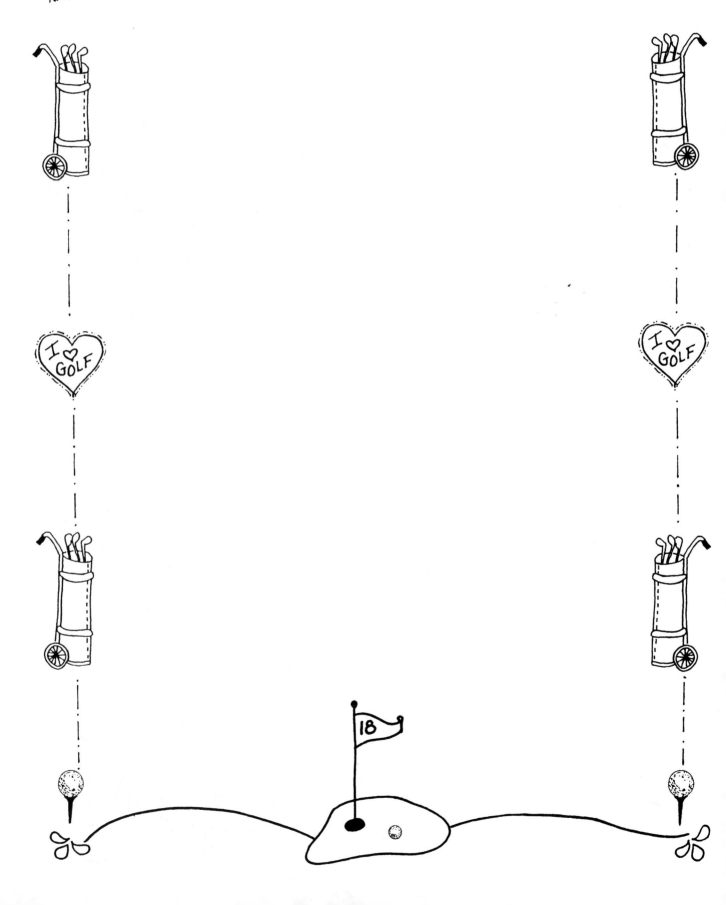

Golf is a ball...no matter how you slice it

Golfing

If I can't be seen, I'm on the green

Ever stop to think...
what golf spells backwards
Al Bolinski

Happiness
is a hole in one

I can still drive 300 yards... in my golf cart

Now that I'm older
I can hit the ball
out of sight

18

Golf or my wife ???
When's tee time?

I'm no TIGER
on the green
because I'm always
in the WOODS!

I WOULD GIVE UP GOLF
IF I DIDN'T HAVE SO MANY
SWEATERS! - Bob Hope

It takes a lot of balls to golf the way I do

GOLF BALL PAR-KING

No matter if you hook or slice,
you're better than par
on the fairway of life

Will Play Golf
for Food!

Coffin Break

Hallowe'en Howls and Pumpgrins

Halloween

STOP for a spell

My other car is a broom

IF the BROOM FITS FLY it

Ghost cards & Fang mail

Tomb it may concern

Witch Way? Fright turn →

Don't Be a Fraidy Cat

Boooo to Youooo

Witchful Thinking

Too Cute To Spook

Hallowe'en Menu
Moanday to Frightday

Ham boogers
Apple spider
Ice Scream
Hallow weiners
Rice creepies
Boo Bury Pie
Fresh Baked Dread
Coffin Drops
Mice Pudding
Foolish goulish
Sticky goo cooked just for you.

Tomb it may concern

Monsters For Sale

Fly our scare plane Ghost to Ghost

Bone Voyage

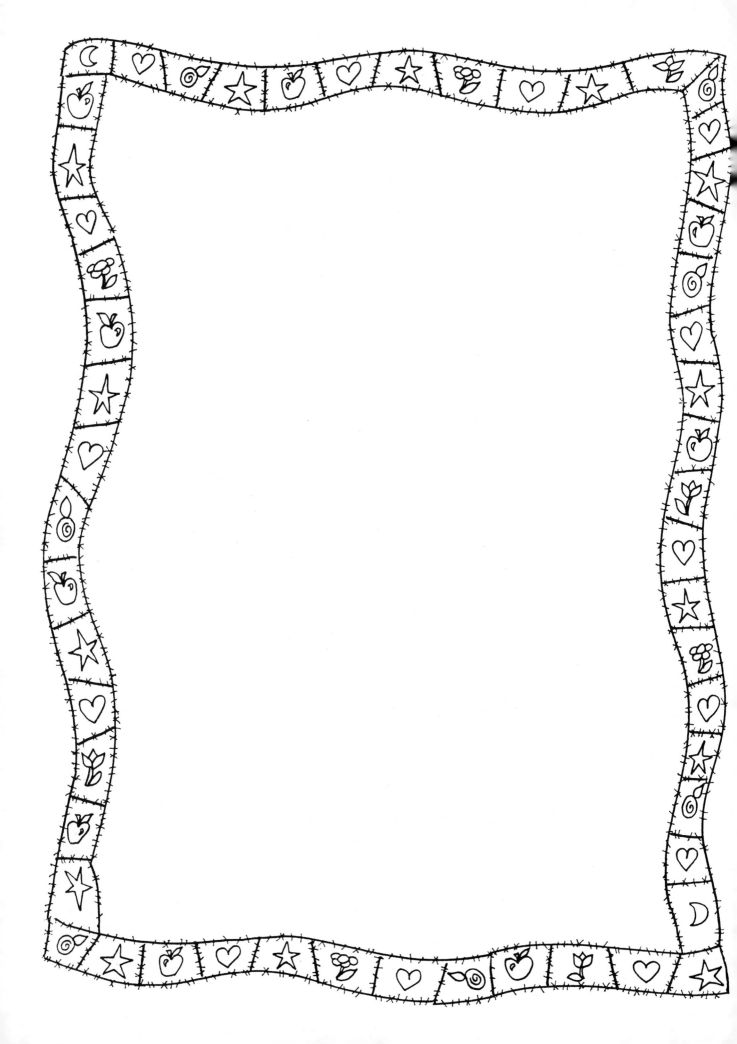

Brains are Soft
Helmets are Hard
Use Both!

BE the change you want to see in the WORLD
Ghandi

THERE WAS NEVER A GOOD WAR OR A BAD PEACE
- Benjamin Franklin

Protect Mother Nature
She's the oldest mom around.

No Smoking
Purdy Please

If you pray for rain ......
be prepared to deal with some mud.

Recycle toucans
or 3 cans
or 4 cans.

She who laughs, lasts
- Norwegian Proverb

Laughter is .....
sunshine in the heart
and wings on the soul

Save our animals
It's a Tall order

HUGS - not drugs

Beauty comes in all sizes

Keep our rainforests
Wet and Wild

POLLUTION
It's a WHALE of a problem.

49

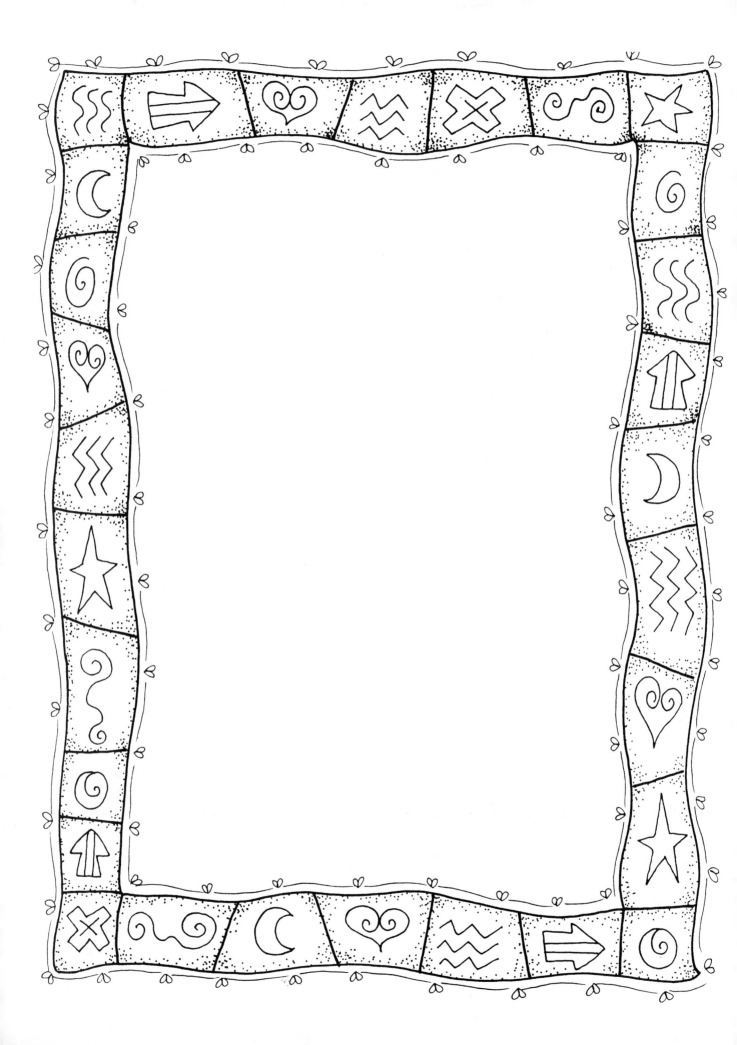

I only craft on days that end with "Y"

All Roads Lead To Crafting
♥ CAUTION ♥
♥ Craftaholic in Residence ♥

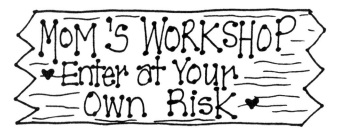
MOM'S WORKSHOP
♥ Enter at Your Own Risk ♥

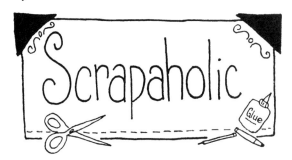
Scrapaholic

♥ Tole fairies workshop ♥

Paint til you faint!

The best gifts are always handmade

My eyes are square cuz I can't quit playing with my software

File not found
Should I fake it?
Yes ___ No ___

If there is No Internet in Heaven... I'm not going!

**Proofread carefully
to see if you any words out**

Smash forehead on Keyboard to continue

51

This scrapbook page is designed
to hold photos of family members,
including pets inside the windows and door.

Home Sweet Home

WELCOME

May Our Home Be Warm
And Our Friends Be Many

HOME

Home is where MOM is!

HOMESPUN

Home Is Where Your Honey Is

CABIN ♥ SWEET ♥ CABIN

Honey

A man travels the world over in search of what he needs and returns home to find it
- George Moore

A house is built with boards & beams
A home is built with love & dreams.

A HAPPY HOME IS FILLED WITH LOVE & LAUGHTER

May Peace Be With You While You Stay & Joy Be With You On Your Way

Home is where the hugs are

Love Begins at Home

Home for the Harvest

Honey Do List:

Attention Spiders - Don't worry
We keep house casually

HOUSEWORK STINKS!

I'd rather live here in our cozy little home stenciled with fingerprints and brimming with love than alone in a sparkling mansion

My idea of housework is to sweep the room with a glance

Laundry Room
Drop your drawers here

Home of a Domestic Goddess

MOTHERHOOD IS LOADS OF FUN

HOUSEWORK STINKS!
DUST

After ecstacy... the laundry

What's a nice girl like me doing in a place like this?

All work & No pay - $ makes a housewife

Housework makes your hare turn gray

STOP Pollution... clean your room!

This isn't clutter these are my priceless antiques

If a man's home is his castle... let him clean it

55

The sky is the limit when your ♡ is in it!

Wish it... Dream it... Do it

Inspiration

We create our tomorrows by what we dream today

We can't all be stars but we can all twinkle.

Happiness is Best Kept When Given Away

What lies behind us and What lies ahead of us Is nothing compared to What lies within us
— Morrow

Beauty is Internal

Don't dream it Be it

Life is like a canvas Make yours a Masterpiece

If it is to Be It's up to Me!

Celebrate LIFE

Those Who Wish To Sing Always Find a Song

To Improve Your Outlook, Keep Looking Up

Happiness is where you find it.

Live Your Life as an Exclamation Not an Explanation!

Improvement begins with I!

The Kitchen is the ♥ of a Home

Bless the Cook who Serves Love and Laughter

Enjoy Life— It's Delicious

Recipe for a Happy Heart
2 cups of love
1 cup of friendship
1 cup of gratitude
Add a dash of laughter
Pour into any soul

Todays Menu
Two Choices...
Take it or Leave it

Bon Appetit

Never trust a skinny cook

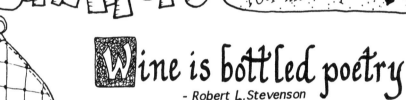
Wine is bottled poetry
- Robert L. Stevenson

THIS IS AN EQUAL OPPORTUNITY KITCHEN EVERYONE COOKS & CLEANS

I cook with wine... sometimes I even put it in food

Real men wear aprons

Dressed to Grill

Only the pure of heart can make good soup
- Ludwig Van Beethoven

Crumbs of happiness make a loaf of contentment

This kitchen is Closed
Due to Illness
I'm sick of cooking

59

This Kitchen is Seasoned with Love

Nothing says lovin' like fresh pie from the oven

Hot Stuff

Coffee or a pot of tea?
Please sit and share
A cup with me.

Friendship hits the spot

Chocolate is an essential nutrient

Love & Scandal
are the best sweeteners of tea.
- Henry Fielding

HOME is where the cookies are.

Nana's Kitchen Tasters Welcome

Mothers add lovin' spoonfuls

Life's Two best comforts Good Food and a HUG

Calling Children strong and able Clear your dishes Off the table

If you want breakfast in bed...
sleep in the kitchen

61

The Present is a Gift

The rest of your Life begins right Here & Now!

Life's Like That

Fate just keeps on happening

How wonderful the little things in life can be

In spite of the cost of living, it's still popular

Humor can make a serious difference

Tell the truth –
There's less to remember

Facts are stubborn things

Practice makes perfect
Just be careful what you practice

A budget:
going broke methodically

The best things in life
are not free, just priceless

BIRTHDAYS are
a gift from God
that's why we can't
return them

There are two ways to be rich.....
make more or desire less

LIFE

Life is nothing like the Brochure

At the Touch of Love Everyone Becomes a Poet

- Plato

No treasure on earth
could ever compare
to the joy we've known
and the love we share

Let's You & I
Dance Barefoot
Under A
Moonlit Sky

You Rock My World!

For all the joy you spread
and thoughtfullness you show
You are loved so much more
than you could ever know.

If I could make all your dreams
come true in every way,
I'd multiply all the gifts of love
you bring me everyday

Love Birds Forever

Love Nest

Live IN MY HEART AND PAY NO Rent

Of all my favourite happy times
so special to recall,
the times we've spent together
are my most cherished of all.

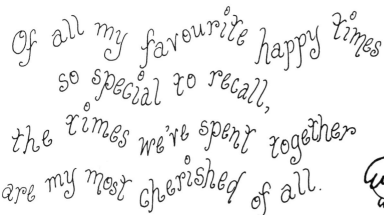

65

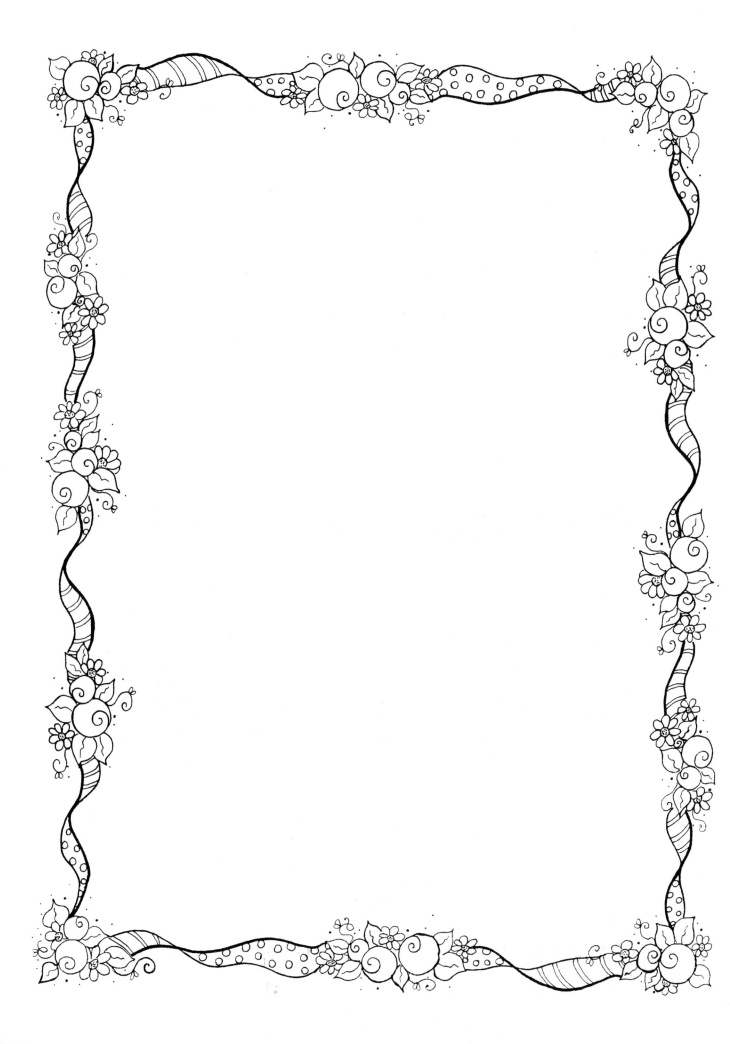

My favorite place is inside your hug

Joined in Heart
May the Two of Us
Never Part

Wishes
for Thee
from little
ol' me

♡-felt wishes
for the new
Mr. & Mrs.

When we love ....
we grow

TWEET ♥ HEART

I want to share my ♡ with you

Happiness is Being Married to Your Best Friend

Homespun
with
LOVE

The secret of love
is to open your ♡

Love
is spoken
Here

♡'s that share =
♡'s that care

Love is the Source of Life

You melt my ♡

We all grow better with love

A hug a day keeps the grumpies away

LOVE

Our policy is to blame the computer

Shop like a bull
Charge everything

To err is human
but it's against
company policy

Our customers are worth a mint to us 🍬

Nurses can really take the pressure and go the rounds

Great DOCTORS
have lots of patience

Nursing is ...
a ♥ work ♥ of ♥ heart

Pharmacists Rx-tra
Special

Give Your Heart
to a Nurse

Secretaries are ...
a special type

Hygienists brighten your day

Hair stylists
are shear pleasure

Firefighters Save
♥'s & Homes

I'm a beautician...not a magician

It's my 40th and I'll cry if I want to

It's my 40th and I'll cry if I want to

It's my 40th and I'll cry if I want to

It's my 40th and I'll cry if I want to

It's hard to be nostalgic...
When you can't remember anything

over the hill

Forget the HOT FLASHES
Give me some POWER SURGES!

I'm much too young to look old

Aged To Perfection

Pushing 50 is exercise enough

Goodbye Tension Hello Pension

I'm not 40 —
I'm 18 with some
extra years of
experience

Too old to work
Too young to die
So off into the sunset
Just me and my.

We ♥ our RV

Me 40!
I demand a recount

Old enough to know better....
Too old to care

We are always the same age inside
— Gertrude Stein

40 happens

It's never too late
to have a happy childhood

Recycled Teenager

We're retired .....
Our job is having a good time

You know you're over the hill
when "happy hour"
means "nap time"

Tales of Treasured Times Together

Little Sugarplum (S)

Once in A Millennium Baby

Sweet Peas

Kickin' OFF A Great Season

Hot Shot

King of the Road

I'm a Collectable Special Edition

Buckaroo Baby

Bathin' Beauties

A Real Hottie!

This is the Life

Photos

A happy memory is a forever joy

Best of Buds

★ Every page has possible photo quips

Photo Quips   clic   clic   clic

A Dream Come True

Superstar

Pretty as a Picture

I'm a Photo-Hugger

Grandma's Little Angels

No Bones About It
I'm Dog-gone Cute

Rugrats in Training

Cool Dude

Super Granny Super Gramps

I'm a Photo-Hugger

Party Animal

I'm stuck on you!

You GO Girl!

If every picture tells a story... this one's a BESTSELLER

75

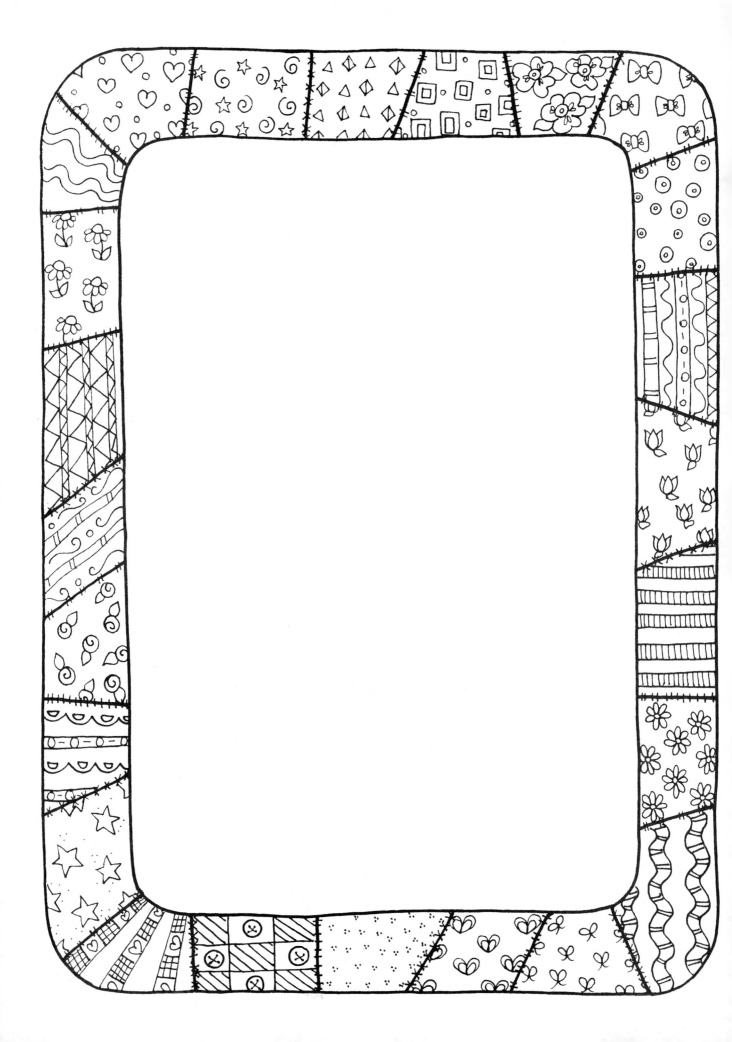

Quilts are patches of love

On the 8th day God created quilts.

Quilters Dream A WORLD PEACED

Days stitched with LOVE rarely unravel

What's Stitched With Love Will Never Tear

All things are mended stitch by stitch.

Life's a Stitch

MOM'S SCISSORS HANDS OFF!   Sewers leave you in stitches!

Don't put all of your spools in one basket

A Quilt is... a Labour of Love

Quilters never come apart at the seams

You can always tell a quilter by the threads she wears.

SEW KINDNESS GATHER LOVE

Love is the thread of life   77

Stitchin & Quiltin

SCHOOL IS COOL

Teachers Make A Difference

Teachers Rule!

Teaching 1+a =

A·B·C

Teachers make the Grade.

A+

KIDS ARE MY BUSINESS

If you want children to excel
let them hear all the nice things you say
about them to others

Teachers make the little ones count 1 2 3 4

Books are food for the brain

EDUCATING THE MIND
WITHOUT EDUCATING THE SOUL
IS NO EDUCATION AT ALL
- Aristotle (384-322 BC)

You can't scare me I teach

The Art of Teaching is the art of Assisting in Discovery

I don't raise 'em ....
I just teach 'em.

To teach is to learn twice
— Joubert

Teachers can't live on apples alone.

School is cool School is cool School is cool School is cool

Dancing is Tu-Tu Much Fun!

Everything In Life I Share
Except Of Course My Teddy Bear

Never Fear Teddy Bears Are Near

Fur Coats Leave Me Cold

Have you hugged your teddy today?

You are Beary Special

LOVE THY TEDDY

Be beary quiet
Baby sleeping

My bear may be old and worn
and tattered all about
but I know my bear still loves me
cuz a bears love can't fall out

Bear bottoms
Welcome Here

Bear-ware
Teddies everywhere

Love Beareth All Things

Grin & Bear it

Have a Beary Merry Christmas

Don't leave this place unbearable

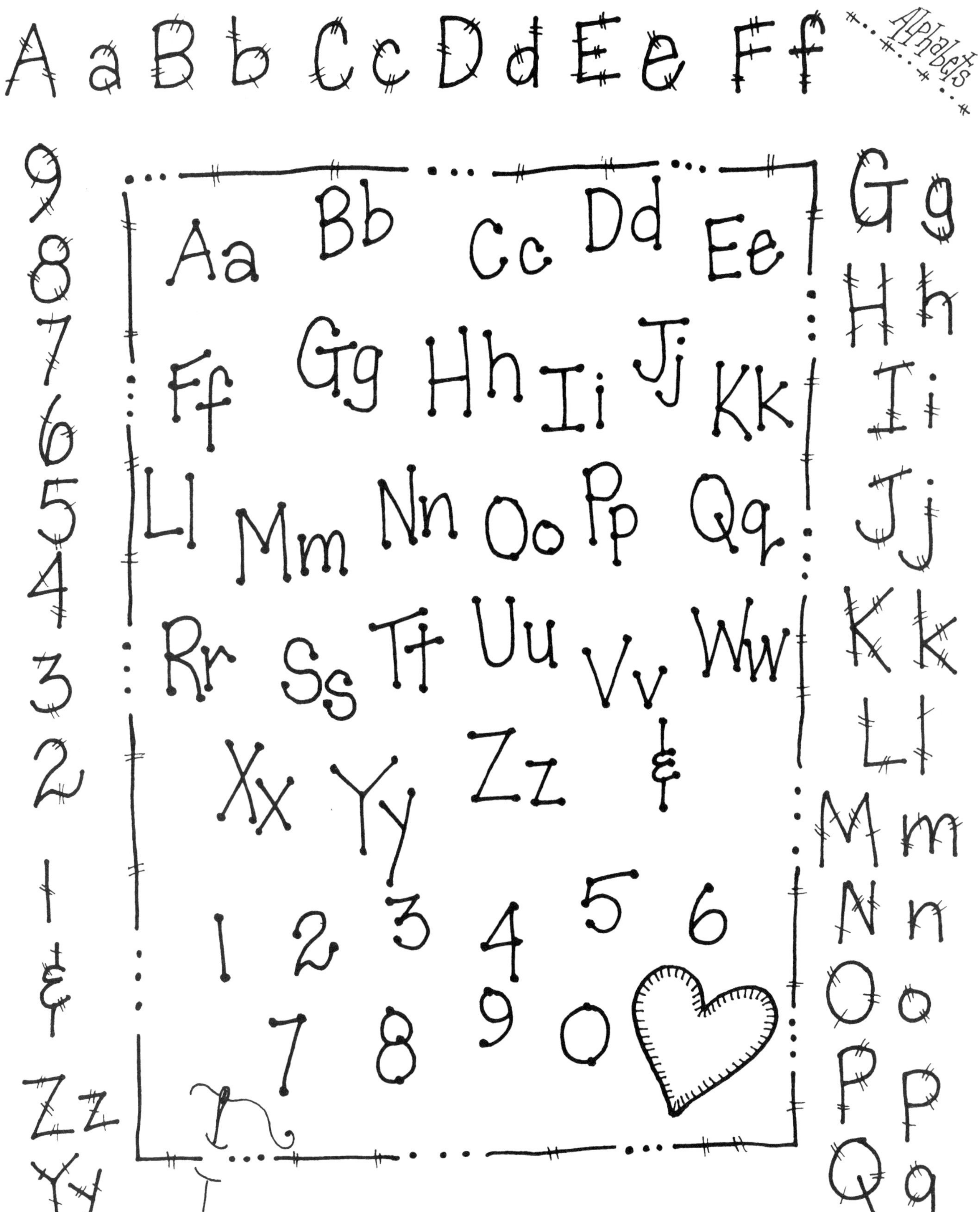

A a B b C c D d E e F f

G g
H h
I i
J j
K k
L l
M m
N n
O o
P p
Q q
R r

9
8
7
6
5
4
3
2
1
&
Z z
Y y
X x

Aa Bb Cc Dd Ee

Ff Gg Hh Ii Jj Kk

Ll Mm Nn Oo Pp Qq

Rr Ss Tt Uu Vv Ww

Xx Yy Zz &

1 2 3 4 5 6

7 8 9 0

W w V v U u T t S s R r

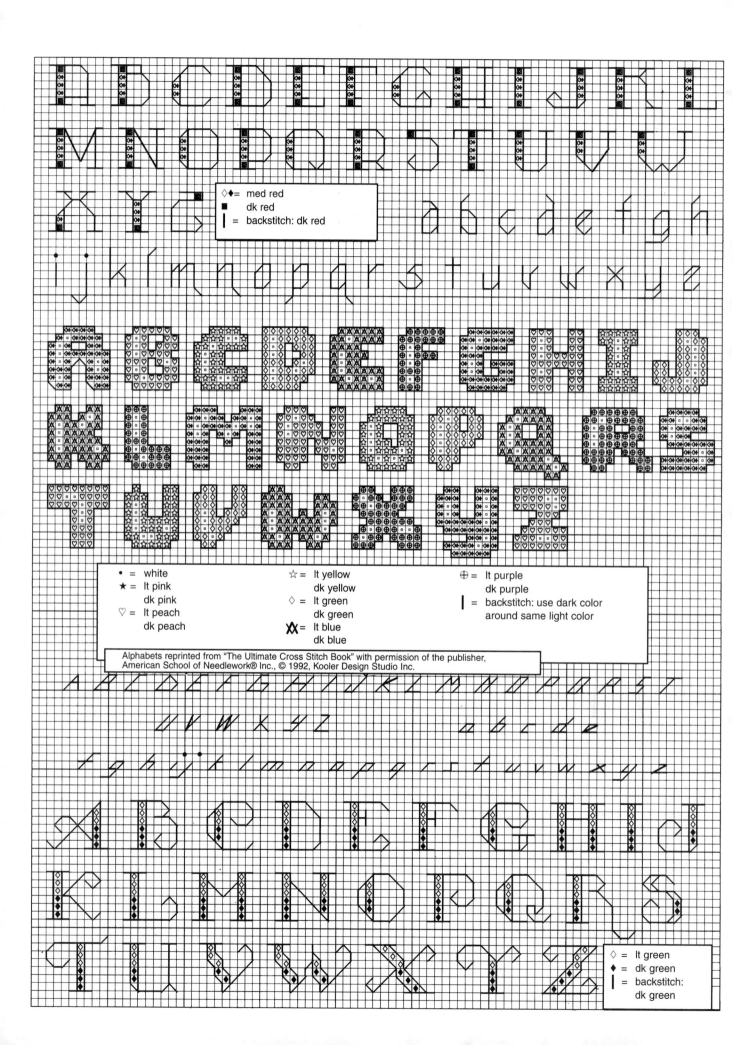

ABCDEFGHIJKLM
NOPQRSTUVW
XYZ

◇♦= med red
■ = dk red
| = backstitch: dk red

abcdefgh
ijklmnopqrstuvwxyz

ABCDEFGHIJ
KLMNOPQRS
UVWXYZ

• = white   ☆ = lt yellow   ⊕ = lt purple
★ = lt pink   dk yellow   dk purple
    dk pink   ◇ = lt green | = backstitch: use dark color
♡ = lt peach   dk green   around same light color
    dk peach   ✗✗ = lt blue
                        dk blue

Alphabets reprinted from "The Ultimate Cross Stitch Book" with permission of the publisher,
American School of Needlework® Inc., © 1992, Kooler Design Studio Inc.

ABCDEFGHIJKLMNOPQRST
UVWXYZ   abcde
fghijklmnopqrstuvwxyz

ABCDEFGHIJ
KLMNOPQRS
TUVWXYZ

◇ = lt green
♦ = dk green
| = backstitch:
    dk green

Aa Bb Cc Dd Ee
Ff Gg Hh Ii Jj Kk
Ll Mm Nn Oo Pp
Qq Rr Ss Tt Uu
Vv Ww Xx Yy Zz

Aa Bb Cc Dd Ee
Ff Gg Hh Ii Jj Kk
Ll Mm Nn Oo Pp
Qq Rr Ss Tt Uu
Vv Ww Xx Yy Zz

85

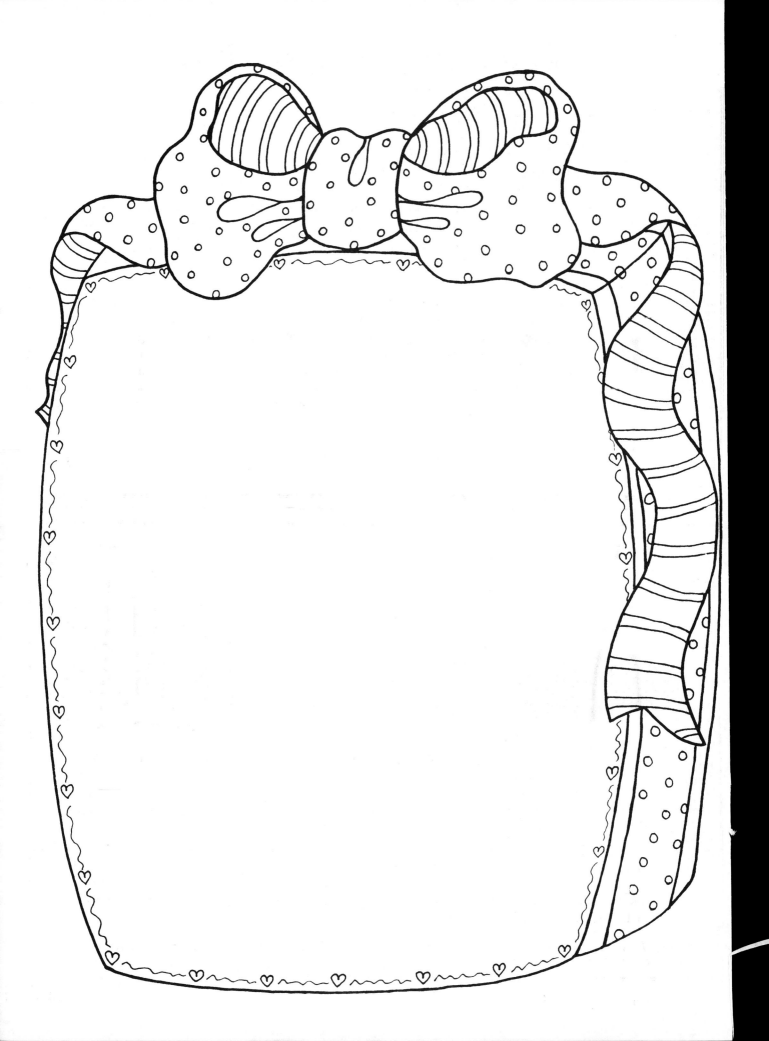

Easy Projects on Pots

Birthday Muffin Pot

Supplies Needed:
- One 4 to 5" Terra-cotta Pot
- Pēbēo Porcelain Paint in a light color
- Pēbēo Porcelain Paint in a dark color
- Pēbēo Black Outliner Pen
- 24" Complimentary Color Ribbon
- Paintbrush and Old Toothbrush

Paint the pot first with any light color following the manufacturer's directions. Once dry, use a tooth brush to lightly spatter paint the pot with a darker color. Trace over the expression pattern and transfer it on the pot using transfer paper. Paint the letters using a black Outliner Pen. This pen comes in a tube and gives a nice, clean, raised line. After oven baking, according to the manufacturer's directions, the finish will be permanent, glossy and non toxic. Tie a ribbon around the pot rim and add a jumbo muffin or cupcake with a candle. Voilà, you have a sweet gift for a friend!

You can choose any color combination for your pot.
Our pot was painted white and spatter painted with burgundy.

Pin Cushion Pot

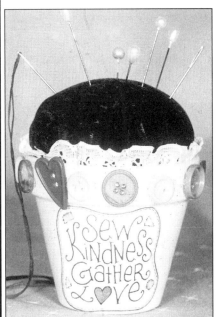

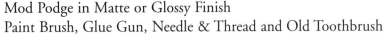

Supplies Needed:
- One 4 to 5 " Terra-cotta Pot
- Acrylic Paints in a light & dark color
- 6" circle of Velvet or Other Fabric
- Fiberfill Stuffing
- 12" of Lace & Asst. Buttons
- Pencil Crayons or Colored Markers
- B&W and Color Photo Copies
- Mod Podge in Matte or Glossy Finish
- Paint Brush, Glue Gun, Needle & Thread and Old Toothbrush

Paint the pot in a light colour. Once dry, spatter paint pot with a complimentary color to the fabric. Using a photocopy of this page, color the large quilt shape in a light color, shading the edges darker. Color the small shapes in the corners and the heart. Have a color copy made and cut the "quilt" out carefully. Using a brush, paint the back with Mod Podge and glue it to the pot, smoothing out any air bubbles. Seal entire pot with a thin coat of Mod Podge. Glue lace around inside of pot rim. Stuff pot with fiberfill. Baste around the fabric circle with thread. Fill circle with fiberfill and pull on the thread to gather fabric. Glue this pincushion "ball" inside the pot. Glue buttons around the pot rim.

You can choose any color combination for your pot. Our pot was painted beige and spattered with green paint. The pin cushion was made from green velvet.

Friendship Pen Pot

Supplies Needed:
>   One 4 to 5" Terra-cotta Pot
>   Acrylic Paints in White and Light Blue
>   One Color Photograph of Best Friends
>   B&W and Color Photocopies, see below
>   Pencil Crayons or Colored Markers
>   Mod Podge in Matte or Glossy Finish
>   6" circle of 1" Grid Mesh Wire
>   Pen with Removable Plastic Plug
>   Green Floral Tape
>   Artificial Daisy and 3 Leaves
>   Paintbrush, Old Toothbrush, Glue Gun

Paint the outside of pot white. Once dry, spatter with light blue paint. Using a photocopy of this page, color the insides of both frames in light blue, shading the edges darker. Color the hearts pink and stars and the inside of the capital letters yellow. Have a color copy made of your work and photograph (photograph can be sized on a color copier and cropped to fit inside the colored frame). Carefully cut out the designs from the colored copies. Use Mod Podge on a brush to glue the border around the pot rim and the framed photo below it, smoothing out any air bubbles. Glue extra stars and hearts randomly around your pot. Seal the whole pot with a thin coat of Mod Podge.

Flower Pen Directions

Remove the plastic plug from the end of a pen and wrap the pen with green floral tape leaving only the metal nib exposed. Cut daisy leaving a 1" stem. Glue leaves to underside of daisy. Glue the daisy and stem into end of your pen.

Snip the edges around the circle of wire mesh and bend them so you can push mesh snugly down into the pot. The 1" grids will hold the pen upright.

More Pen Pot Ideas

Pen pots are an easy and inexpensive gift to make. Poinsettias , roses and sunflower pens teamed with the right expression make great gifts for teachers, Mother's day, birthdays and more. Flower pens are also perfect in an office or store, where people often walk away with the pens by accident.